The Prestige Series

Trent 2

John Banks

Photography by G H

© 2004 Venture Publications Ltd

ISBN 1 898432 99 6

Cover: Trent's last new Bristol VRs had been delivered in 1981. The replacement Leyland Olympian appeared in the Trent fleet with a batch of seven in 1983. Of the batch 700-6, No. **705** (**XAU 705Y**) was still very new when photographed in Mansfield Road, Nottingham, in August 1983.

Rear cover: Trent's timetable in 1960 was rather plain and lacked even a sketch of a bus or coach on its covers. With 224 pages and a fold-out map, however, it was good value at sixpence (2½p).

Inside covers: A selection of the liveries that have been seen on Trent vehicles in the period covered by this book: Leyland PD3 No. **401** (**LRC 435**), seen at Derby in August 1965, carries the traditional red and ivory so familiar for many years in the pre-National Bus Company period; the National Bus Company's poppy-red and white is displayed on another Titan, 1957's PD2/12 No. **779** (**KCH 122**), also at Derby; Bristol VR No. **838** (**BRC 838T**) is in the post-NBC subdued red and silver of the late 1980s; and the Ayres red and cream that followed around 1991/2 is shown on No. **619** (**G619 OTV**), an Alexander-bodied Volvo B10M-50, of 1989.

Title page: Willowbrook and AEC Regent were virtually synonymous in the Trent fleet across the five years 1946-50. Even after orders for new vehicles were transferred 100% to Leyland in 1951 as long as the AECs lasted they maintained a high profile in the fleet. Typical of them was No. **1152** (**ACH 642**), a 1948 example.

Opposite page: As so often in this series of books featuring the photography of Geoffrey Atkins, the bus stations in Nottingham feature prominently, none more so than that in Huntingdon Street. In this peaceful January 1953 view one of Trent's earliest underfloor-engined service buses, Leyland Royal Tiger **808** (**DCH 908**), was waiting to leave for Chesterfield on the 63, jointly operated with East Midland Motor Services. In the inset is Trent's enthusiastic publicity for its 1997 "Best Bus Company" award in the rear window of No. **238** (**P238 CTV**), an Optare Metrorider.

Below: In 1972 Trent's fleet was not yet wholly devoid of traditional front-engined double-deckers, but the rear-engined revolution meant that none had been bought new since1958. In this view at Nottingham Victoria in August of that year, rear-engined vehicles are prominent. The sole traditional double-decker, at the end of the row, was in the Barton fleet. The photographer annotated the back of the original of this print "a mixed bag". Indeed.

INTRODUCTION

Before the National Bus Company

Volume One of this work, published by Venture Publications Ltd in early 2004, took the story from Trent's humble beginnings as staff transport for a country estate at Ashbourne in 1913 through a remarkable period of growth and consolidation in the twenties and thirties, through the dark days of the Second World War and up to the dawn of the postwar period of austerity and shortages.

Peace brought relief to a war-weary country and both military and civilian arms could look forward to much-needed respite from the awfulness of war. Few would have realised - or have believed it had they been told - that the period of austerity, rationing and general difficulty would last longer than had the war.

The bus operators were faced with a dichotomous situation: there was great demand for their services; few people owned cars, television was practically unknown, and the need for buses, and plenty of them, was paramount, not only for people travelling to and from work, but also for shopping and leisure activities such as visits to the cinema. On the other hand, to meet this demand operators had

fleets that were mostly prewar in origin, or of utility design and wartime manufacture using - especially in the case of bodywork - heavy and sometimes poor quality materials, the use of unseasoned "green" timber being a major cause of later problems.

New buses in anything like the quantities needed to replace time-served, war-battered fleets were not immediately available in 1945, and what there were went mainly for export, the earning of foreign exchange being a priority of the new Labour government - "Export or Die" was the slogan. Matters improved gradually and by 1950 most operators had restocked with new, rebodied or substantially rebuilt vehicles with which to cater for the passenger boom of that decade.

Thus the fleet took on a new look. In 1942 Trent had passed under the wing of the British Electric Traction Company at the time of the great BET/Tilling split. Prewar, its fleet had been virtually synonymous with the Midland Red-built SOS chassis, although Daimler and AEC made inroads in the late thirties.

In the immediate postwar period, regardless of the presence in it of other *marques*, Trent's was "an AEC fleet", certainly to the writer, in the same way that Hull Corporation ran "an AEC fleet" despite its Guys and Leylands, and

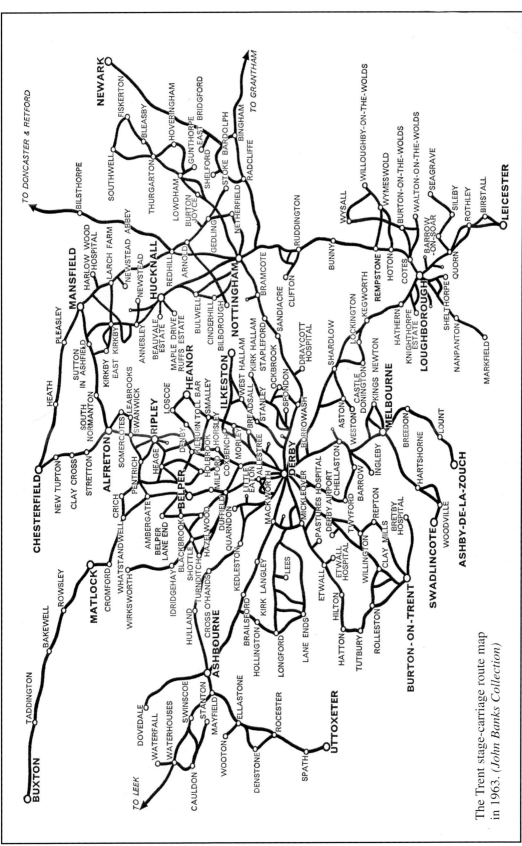

The Trent stage-carriage route map in 1963. (*John Banks Collection*)

- conversely - that East Yorkshire was in the mind's eye "a Leyland fleet", an identity not overly affected by - again - Guys, as well as AECs. Although Trent took delivery of Daimlers in 1945, these were the aftermath of allocations made by the wartime Ministry of War Transport and Ministry of Supply arrangements. For the rest of the decade, from the first full year of peace - 1946 - to the end of 1950, in fact, nothing but AEC Regals and Regents was purchased. There was remarkable homogeneity, too, in the orders for new bodywork for these AECs: apart from a handful of coaches from Windover, everything was bodied locally by Willowbrook.

In 1951 there was a big swing to Leyland and for the next decade and more, little else was bought: a few AEC Reliances serving only to make the Lancashire manufacturer's domination seem the more complete.

The fifties were a good time for Trent, as they were for most other bus operators, and the Company prospered, introducing summer services to a variety of seaside resorts as well as a non-stop service between Nottingham and Derby operated jointly with Barton Transport.

In the sixties, with rear-engined, front-entrance double-deckers becoming popular for a variety of stated reasons that all boiled down to a desire to ease recruitment problems and save money by doing away with conductors, Leyland was again present in the fleet with the Atlantean although Daimler made much progress with the Fleetline and a number of lightweight Bedfords was purchased.

In 1963, the year of the Company's Golden Jubilee, the fleet stood at 390, made up of 156 single-deckers, 195 double-deckers and 39 coaches. Comparative figures for 1927 are 150 vehicles (119, 13 and 18).

All those new 1960s vehicles came into a fleet that was now serving a declining demand. The decade was a good deal less successful as those two curses of the public-transport provider, television and the private car, began to lay their grip on the population. Passenger numbers fell and the network was reduced - a classic example of the "use it or lose it" syndrome that has been repeated so many times then and since. The Company still strove to cope with the changing profile of its business, however, holiday tours being an example. In

1929 Trent advertised five tours; in 1963 there were twelve, the most ambitious being 13 days to the Highlands. This successful side of the Company's activities were soon to suffer at the hands of a new management, as mentioned later in these jottings.

A highlight of the decade was the opening of a new depot at Meadow Road, Derby. Two new garage buildings and the conversion of an existing garage combined to give parking and docking facilities for 161 vehicles.

In March 1968, the British Electric Traction Company sold its bus interests to the Government-owned Transport Holding Company. The BET had owned 41.2% of the shares in the Trent Motor Traction Co. Ltd, and an equivalent percentage had been already owned by the THC via its former railway interests. The remaining 17.6% were in private hands, in some cases going back to the formation of the Company.

The National Bus Company and Beyond

On 1st January 1969, the formation of the National Bus Company resulted in the equation BET + THC = NBC. In fact, it was not quite as simple as that, for the Joint Omnibus Committees in Yorkshire were also involved and in the same year were created four Passenger Transport Authorities and Passenger Transport Executives. Of the latter, Trent was affected by the prolix South East Lancashire and North East Cheshire Passenger Transport Executive, commonly known as SELNEC, which had taken over the passenger transport activities of ten municipalities in the Greater Manchester area.

The main NBC operator in the southern part of SELNEC's area was the Stockport-based North Western Road Car Co. Ltd, which ran services in Greater Manchester, Cheshire and Derbyshire.

In 1971 agreement was reached for North Western to split and sell its stage carriage operation among SELNEC, Crosville Motor Services Ltd of Chester, and Trent. This left North Western as an operator of express services only. The NBC was attempting to fit operators to counties, with Crosville responsible for Cheshire and Trent looking after Derbyshire.

As a consequence, in 1972 Trent purchased, for just over a quarter of a million pounds, North Western garages at Buxton, Castleton and Matlock; 48 vehicles and five chassis awaiting bodies; and two Land Rovers. Fifty-five assorted stage, works and schools services were taken over, as well as the excursion and tour licences from Buxton, Hayfield, Matlock and Darley Dale.

NBC policy was to merge smaller companies into neighbouring larger ones and Trent assumed management responsibility for the Midland General Omnibus Co. Ltd on 1st April 1972. MGOC was operated as a separate concern until 1976, when it was fully integrated into Trent.

Early in 1972 Trent started a renumbering programme for the vehicles acquired from North Western and in April of that year renumbered the routes to avoid duplication. More renumbering of vehicles in September 1972 saw the Midland General fleet merged into the Trent numbering series, although at that time the Midland General fleetname did not disappear. Enthusiasts soon noticed interesting vehicle movements, with Midland

General buses appearing at Matlock and Derby depots.

As might be expected of an NBC operator, many Leyland Leopard coaches entered the fleet. Bristol VR double-deckers and RE single-deckers, and then Leyland National single-deckers began to appear as the Company settled down under the new régime.

Further upheaval in 1973 saw Trent's long distance services pass under the umbrella control of the newly formed National Travel (NBC) Ltd, as the result of transferring them to National Travel (Midlands) Ltd - which was the old South Midland Motor Services Ltd, of Oxford, renamed. Ironically, the latter was short of vehicles, so Trent carried on working its own services and was paid a fixed mileage charge for so doing.

A further - and unfortunate - change affected Trent's extended tour programme. In 1967 ten thousand passengers had been carried on tours throughout Great Britain and by 1971 this had increased to eleven thousand. The NBC's idea was to operate a holiday programme combining the activities in this sphere of 16 companies into one brochure. Not

*Trent at the beginning of the prosperous decade of the 1950s in a typical streetscape at Mount Street, Nottingham. This November 1951 view of the proud and smartly attired crew of No. 200 (**CRC 510**), a Leyland Royal Tiger PSU1/15 coach with centre-entrance 41-seat bodywork, also by Leyland, includes much other detail that is redolent of the 1950s, from the prewar miniature sports car and the stylish Ford 10 across the road to the Midland General AEC Regent and Barton utility Guy Arab further along the street. The Trent vehicle had been new earlier that year as part of a batch of ten. It had just arrived in Nottingham from Skegness.*

surprisingly, this proved impossible, and five area brochures were produced, of which the Midlands Area involved Trent, Midland Red, South Midland, and the newly acquired independent Worthington Tours, of Wolverhampton. Combined passenger totals were 47,300 in 1971 and 12,120 in 1977 - a 74% decrease. Although Trent may have supplied vehicles for the National Holidays programme, it no longer had any say in the organisation and operation of the tours. The holidaying public needed a while to restore its confidence in the new product and by 1985 National Holidays had become a major force in the coach holiday market.

A serious overnight fire at Meadow Road Garage, Derby, resulted in the total loss of or serious damage to 42 vehicles in July 1976. Other companies moved vehicles into Derby and no service mileage was lost the next morning. Strange fleetnames operating Trent services as a result of this exercise included Midland Red, East Midland, Lincolnshire and West Yorkshire; vehicles from the Derby and Nottingham municipal fleets also took part. As if that were not enough, fire struck Manvers Street Garage, Nottingham, in the same year, and a further two vehicles were lost.

Nineteen-seventy-six also saw the Trent garage in Alfreton closed and its vehicles moved to the town's former Midland General depot in King Street.

Signalling an important change of operating policy and outlook, in 1977 discussions took place among Trent, the City of Derby and Derbyshire County Council in connection with a tripartite operating agreement. In later years, coordination in Nottinghamshire, involving Trent, East Midland Motor Services, the Lincolnshire Road Car Company, City of Nottingham Transport, the independents Barton Transport and W Gash, as well as British Rail, brought about the Sherwood Forest Network, which included joint operation of routes that had been the sole preserve of one or other of the constituents. These wide-ranging changes were implemented over a two-year period into 1979.

Two limited stop services to Manchester - the X1 from Derby and the X2 from Nottingham - had been taken over by National Travel in 1973. By 1979 they had had so many

alterations that they bore no resemblance to the original routes and in January 1979 Trent introduced two replacement services, the 200 Manchester - Nottingham and the 201 Manchester - Derby. They did not operate in this form for long, both losing their extension to Stockport and Manchester: the 200 then ran from Nottingham to Matlock and the 201 from Derby to Macclesfield.

In 1981, Jim Berresford, of Cheddleton, well known to enthusiasts for the varied selection of vehicles he operated, applied for a licence under his subsidiary company Byrne Brothers, of Leek, for a service between Derby and Manchester, to be numbered X1 and called the "Derbyman", to replace the withdrawn 201. This application caused Trent and Crosville to operate a similar service. Rather unusually, licences for both were granted and they operated as stage carriage. Byrne Brothers started theirs on 9th November 1981: not to be outdone, the Trent/Crosville commenced on the 8th. The competing services were an endless source of problems and infighting and Byrne Bros withdrew in late 1983.

In 1982 the Monopolies and Mergers Commission reported on an investigation into four bus operators, one of which was Trent. The Commission found that there was no abuse of any monopoly situation nor was there any activity being pursued that operated against the public interest. The report also stated that cross-subsidisation provided support for socially necessary services that might otherwise be withdrawn or have to be supported out of public funds.

In 1984, Brian King, formerly Traffic Manager of Ribble Motor Services Ltd, became Trent's General Manager. Having had the unpleasant task in 1980 of closing Ribble's Manchester depot, in October 1984 Mr King introduced a joint-with-Ribble service, the 252 Nottingham and Manchester via Derby.

Vehicle strength was 385 in 1983 and 381 in 1986 - remarkably consistent when compared with 1963's total of 390.

The Transport Act, 1985 brought about deregulation of bus services together with the break-up of the NBC for sale to private enterprise. The Act came into force on 26th October, 1986 - a date that became known as "D-Day". Operators could henceforth work any service, but each had to make a profit and cross-subsidisation was not allowed, despite the 1982 M&MC report mentioned above. The opportunity was taken to withdraw services that were not commercially viable in the hope that County Councils or PTEs would subsidise them: a situation typically illustrated by the 201 and 252 services. The 201 was withdrawn by Crosville/Trent and was put out to tender by Cheshire, Staffordshire and Derbyshire County Councils: over the next 16 years it was operated by six different companies; the 252, a commercial service, which it remains today as the TransPeak, lost Ribble as joint operator, leaving Trent in sole charge.

On 30th December 1986, Trent became the 13th NBC company to be sold, a proposed management buyout led by Brian King having proved successful.

The fleetname was changed to "Trent Buses". A depot was opened in Glossop after Trent won some contracts from the Greater Manchester PTE. This depot was in the yard of the Dinting Railway Centre. Following refusal by the local council for the building of a proper depot, this operation was transferred to Buxton garage. Staff objected to this and refused to travel to Buxton, so Trent withdrew, being replaced on most of the affected routes by East Midland in 1987.

Trent joined the minibus movement in 1988 when its first - Carlyle-bodied Ivecos - were delivered. In July 1989, Wellglade, the holding company for Trent, purchased Barton Transport, which was to be operated as a separate organisation.

In recent times Trent's flair for publicity has been notable: the "Rainbow" routes and "The Spondon Flyer" being prime examples. The 252 was given a facelift as the R1 in the "Rainbow" series, later becoming the "Trans Peak", its specially painted vehicles adding a touch of glamour. The 199 Buxton to Stockport became another high-flyer when it was extended to Manchester Airport as part of the "Skyline" services to the airport.

Brian King could often be seen travelling about on the Company's vehicles: his hands-on management style did much to propel the Company towards its 1997 award as the UK's best bus company. Later in 1997, the Company's Head Office was moved from Derby to the former Midland General premises at Langley Mill.

On 30th January 1998 Trent returned to operating in Loughborough when it purchased the Kinch operation; in March of that year Wellglade commenced operating a separate unit, formally entitled the Notts & Derby Traction Co. Ltd, initially putting into it ten Leyland Nationals and two Olympians. This was a vehicle-owning company only, staff and management being provided by Derby Integrated Transport Services (DITS), with the fleetname "Blue Apple". It exists at the time of writing, but is now an employing company, with an operational fleet of 45, having always had second-hand vehicles from Trent.

The main fleet in recent times has obviously reflected the descent into almost oblivion of the British bus-building industry, with AEC, Bedford, Bristol, Daimler and Leyland among the names that have disappeared. In the nineties many second-hand Leyland Nationals were acquired, some for spare parts only, but many were re-engined and refurbished. DAF, Dennis, Mercedes, Optare, Scania and Volvo have featured among purchases of new vehicles. Double-deckers have not been bought for some years: the last seem to have been some 84-seat Alexander-bodied Volvos in 1988.

The pages that follow present an illustrated survey of most types operated since 1945. The book is, however, neither a definitive history nor a fleet list. To readers anxious to know more about Trent in the postwar period, David Bean's *Trent Part Two, 1946 - 1968*, published in 2002 by Robin Hood Publishing, is highly recommended.

The writer has received generous help from Keith Healey and Ron Maybray in the preparation of this book; David Bean and Alan Oxley have vetted and improved both text and captions; Dave and Mary Shaw have checked the proofs. Grateful thanks to all.

Photographs not otherwise attributed were taken by G H F Atkins and are copyright of the John Banks Collection.

John Banks
Romiley, Cheshire
August 2004

Above: Six 1938 Daimler COG5SDs with Duple 31-seat coach bodies, Nos 637-42, were rebodied by Willowbrook in 1942 as double-deckers. The Duple bodies were stored until 1946 when they were placed on new AEC Regal chassis, RC 8740-5, which retained the same fleet numbers. The example illustrated above, at the Lawn Motor Park, Skegness, in July 1949, was No. **638** (**RC 8741**).

Below: The offside angle of these handsome vehicles is displayed by No. **641** (**RC 8744**), photographed on private hire work. *(The Omnibus Society)*

Above: Although there had been Daimler double-deckers delivered after the end of the war in 1945, they were to wartime utility design. The first true postwar double-deckers were 13 Willowbrook-bodied 56-seat AEC Regents in 1946. Photographed in October of that year at Huntingdon Street, Nottingham, was No. **1120** (**RC 8918**), which had been turned out in the all-red livery that had been introduced to combat wartime materials shortages.

Below: Number **1140** (**RC 9656**), shown in the postwar standard livery, was one of a dozen similar Regents delivered in 1947.

Above: The standard early postwar single-deck service bus also came from AEC, in the shape of the Regal with front-entrance bodywork from Willowbrook. As with the Regents, delivery of the first examples spread across 1946/7. Number **764** (**RC 9670**) was one of the 1947 deliveries.

Below: AEC Regals and Regents appeared in some quantity again in 1948, including some lowbridge examples. Willowbrook again supplied the bodywork for these 55-seaters, represented when brand new by No. **1323** (**ACH 655**). *(John Banks Collection/Willowbrook)*

Above: Among the 1948 deliveries of double-deckers were further highbridge 56-seaters. In another picture of a pristine, just-built vehicle, No. **1156 (ΛCH 646)** is illustrated. *(Senior Transport Archive/Willowbrook)*

Below: The Willowbrook-bodied AECs soon became the high-profile "face" of the early postwar Trent fleet, although it would be some time before all the prewar SOS and wartime Daimler vehicles were withdrawn. **ACH 634**, fleet number **1144** and another of the 1948 highbridge buses, features in a typical Mount Street, Nottingham, scene, in this case from June 1950.

Above: The lowbridge version of the 1948 AEC Regent/Willowbrook combination in service. Passengers alight from No. **1327** (**ACH 659**) in Glasshouse Street, Nottingham, in August 1948. The vehicle had arrived from Chesterfield on the 63 service, operated jointly with East Midland, and the conductor had already turned the side blind for the return journey.

Below: New postwar coaches arrived in 1948 on AEC Regal chassis with handsome Windover coachwork. Of a batch of twelve, eight were 30-seaters when new and four had 32 seats. Number **610** (**ACH 440**) was one of the latter. It was at Mount Street, Nottingham, in April 1950.

Above: There were no new vehicles in 1949, and in 1950 the first Trent 8ft-wide buses appeared when a batch of ten AEC Regent III models was delivered. As might have been expected, they were Willowbrook-bodied 56-seaters, but the chassis were unusual in being the 9621X variant, with Crossley gearboxes. The second of the batch, No. **1201** (**BRC 401**), was in York Street, Nottingham, in September 1954, passing a Southall contemporary in the shape of a magnificent AEC Mammoth Major 8 brewery lorry, **NGF 403**, in the Whitbread fleet.

Below: Single-deckers in 1950 were dual-purpose 33-seaters from Willowbrook on AEC Regal 6821X chassis, again with Crossley gearboxes. The first of 20, No. **100** (**BRC 300**), is shown.

TRENT

MOTOR TRACTION CO. LTD.

<< Opposite page: One of the 1950 dual-purpose single-deckers, No. **105** (**BRC 305**), was used in this advertisement, seen in Victoria railway station, Nottingham, in November 1953. The message was quite subtle - without the need for text - suggesting that the commuter use Trent buses between home and the station.

Above: Crystal-clear detail of entrance and seating layout of the dual-purpose 33-seaters in a shot of No. **114** (**BRC 314**), brand new and before delivery to Trent. *(John Banks Collection/Willowbrook)*

Below: A portrait of one of the 1950 8ft-wide AEC Regents, No. **1205** (**BRC 405**), at Matlock bus station circa 1954.

Above: Number **1205** (**BRC 405**) again, in a typical low-angled Geoffrey Atkins shot designed to highlight the curvaceous lines of the Willowbrook bodywork.

Below: A similar angle for the offside-front view, helped by the downhill slope of Kent Street, Nottingham. Number **1202** (**BRC 402**) was photographed in July 1950 waiting in Kent Street before moving on to Mount Street bus station to take up a timing on service 8 to Derby.

After five years of uninterrupted AEC purchases Trent made an equally exclusive commitment to Leyland in 1951 that lasted until 1959. Normally such a change can be explained by the arrival of a new General Manager or Chief Engineer, but that was not the case here and it is not easy to explain the sudden and complete switch of allegiance, especially as the Company had had little or no previous experience with the Lancashire *marque*. Among the earliest results were the first Trent underfloor-engined vehicles: Leyland-bodied Royal Tiger centre-entrance 41-seat coaches, epitomised by No. **202** (**CRC 512**), in one of Geoffrey Atkins's spectacular night scenes, at Huntingdon Street bus station in December 1953 *(above)*, and No. **207** (**CRC 517**) at Lower Mosley Street, Manchester, about to leave for Derby on the X1 in May 1952.

The Leyland revolution produced all-Leyland double-deckers, of which the first - in 1951 - were PD2/3 Titan highbridge 56-seaters with open rear platforms. Six were delivered, and we see No. **1221** (**CCH 621**), brand new in March 1951, at Sherwood *(above)* on the Nottingham to Mansfield service 62 Direct Route, and *(below)* the same vehicle two years or so later, in March 1954, heading out of Nottingham at Derby Road, Lenton Abbey, being followed by a prewar Austin 10 saloon with a fine Riley, also prewar, going the other way.

Above: The 1951 Leyland Titans were certainly unlike anything that had gone before, and are thought to be the first Leyland double-deckers owned by the Company. This fine portrait of No. **1234** (**CRC 834**), of the second batch, delivered in 1952, emphasises, when compared with the similarly composed picture on page 13 of the Willowbrook AEC Regent, how much variety and individuality there was in that era in designs for a standard service bus.

Below: The Titans in 1952 were 58-seaters, still Leyland-bodied, on the PD2/12 chassis. The year also saw more Leyland-bodied Royal Tigers, this time as 44-seat front-entrance service buses. One of each of the year's deliveries stand side by side at Derby bus station. Number **1228** (**CRC 828**) was awaiting its timing for Nottingham on service 8 and No. **801** (**DCH 901**) was departing for Ockbrook on the 12.

Above: The Leyland 44-seat service bus bodywork was to a rather austere design but was functional and efficient, as was the Royal Tiger chassis, though the latter was somewhat over-engineered and heavy, and was soon replaced by the Tiger Cub. Trent's No. **805 (DCH 905)** typifies the type in its first year of service in this October 1952 view.

Below: In 1952 the PD2/12 Titan 58-seaters came with platform doors but were otherwise very similar to the previous year's vehicles. This splendid panorama of Trent vehicles at Derby bus station in June 1954 stars No. **1238 (DRC 938)**.

Above: The new Leylands of the early 1950s seemed to inspire the photographer to compose some of the finest of his all too few traffic scenes. In this June 1956 view at Mansfield Road, Carrington, No. **1250** (**DRC 950**) was on its way to Retford on the 80, a service operated jointly with East Midland. Postwar affluence was evident in the new Ford Consul emerging from Hucknall Road and the Morris Minor in Magdala Road, as well as the Hillman Minx and the Morris Oxford following the bus. A Nottingham City Transport AEC Regent was in the background.

Below: There were surely sighs of relief at Willowbrook when Trent returned to the fold with an order for six centre-entrance 41-seat coach bodies to be mounted on Leyland Royal Tiger chassis. The batch is illustrated in a view of No. **215** (**ECH 215**) at Huntingdon Street.

Above: In 1954/5 the new Leyland Tiger Cub lightweight model was making its presence felt and Trent took 44-seat service bus examples with Saunders Roe or Weymann bodywork and dual-purpose vehicles bodied by Willowbrook. The SARO and Weymann designs were to become very familiar in BET fleets for the BET, with its vast buying power, placed large orders and the types appeared in many fleets. This SARO example for Trent was No. **818** (**FCH 18**), seen at Derby bus station in September 1955.

Below: The plainer Weymann version, at the same place and in the same month, is illustrated by No. **820** (**FCH 20**).

Above: Further Leyland-bodied PD2/12 Titans with platform doors appeared in 1955. There was snow on the ground in February 1955 at Redhill as No. **1252 (FRC 952)** was being overtaken by a SARO-bodied Tiger Cub, **ORR 355**, of East Midland.

Below: The same bus, the following month, at Huntingdon Street bus station. The back of Geoffrey Atkins's original print has an interesting note to the effect that this was the first stationary bus taken at 1/100th of a second instead of the hitherto standard 1/25th. The photographer confided to me that, at the age of 43, he was finding it harder to control things at the slower shutter speed and thereafter always used the higher, even for stationary vehicles.

Above: The Willowbrook-bodied dual-purpose 41-seaters were very attractive. Here is 1955's brand new No. **129** (**GRC 129**) at Huntingdon Street in June of that year on the X7 to Great Yarmouth. This vehicle was withdrawn in 1967.

Below: While service buses and dual-purpose vehicles on the Tiger Cub chassis were appearing in 1955 with SARO, Weymann and Willowbrook bodies, yet another supplier - Burlingham - was contracted to produce coachwork for some front-entrance 37-seaters in 1955. They were to the popular and stylish Seagull design and are represented by No. **221** (**GRC 221**) in June 1955, about to leave Huntingdon Street on the X5 to Cleethorpes.

Above: Every so often, with a coachwork design that particularly appealed to him, Geoffrey Atkins would take a detailed view, such as this one of 1956's Willowbrook-bodied Leyland Tiger Cub No. **151** (**HRC 151**). The vehicle was a dual-purpose 41-seater.

Below: The closure of Leyland's body plant has never been fully explained, though industrial relations undoubtedly had much to do with it. Metropolitan-Cammell Carriage and Wagon bodywork was specified for Trent's 1956 PD2/12 Titans. There were 59-seat highbridge and 55-seat lowbridge versions, both with platform doors. Number **1260** (**JCH 260**), seen in Derby Road, Nottingham, in May 1956, was one of the highbridge vehicles.

Above: Here is the lowbridge version of the MCCW-bodied PD2/12. Number **1354 (JCH 354)** was photographed at Westgate, Mansfield, in July 1956.

Below: Nine vehicles were acquired from E Naylor and Sons, of Normanton, in July 1956. The oldest was 1932 AEC Regent **VO 8566**, which became Trent No. **1218**. The vehicle had been new to Mansfield District with Weymann bodywork and had passed to Naylor in 1946. A Burlingham 56-seat highbridge body was fitted by Naylor in 1949. The bus survived in Trent service until 1959. It was photographed at Stockwell Gate, Mansfield, in September 1956.

Above: The Naylor acquisition included two Guy Arabs - like Leyland when it first appeared in the fleet, a type with which Trent's operating and engineering staff would have been unfamiliar. Number **1300** (**JNU 796**) was a Gardner five-cylinder-engined Arab II model, with Strachans utility lowbridge 55-seat bodywork. At first numbered 1216 by Trent, it was also withdrawn in 1959. The photograph dates from September 1957 at Derby bus station.

Below: The other Guy was an Arab III model fitted with a Gardner six-cylinder engine and a Northern Coachbuilders 56-seat highbridge body. A 1948 vehicle, **MNU 777** became Trent No. **1217** and was again a 1959 withdrawal. In December 1956, it featured in another Derby bus station view.

Above: Whereas the 1955 Burlingham Seagull coachwork on Leyland Tiger Cubs had been to front-entrance specification, further such vehicles in 1957 were to 37-seat centre-entrance configuration. Number **227** (**KCH 227**), one of a batch of seven, was outside the Barton duty inspector's and parcels office at Huntingdon Street in September 1958.

Below: In 1958 the first 30ft-long double-deckers appeared, on Leyland Titan PD3/4 chassis fitted with Willowbrook 73-seat bodywork with platform doors. From a batch of 22, we illustrate No. **1042** (**LRC 442**) at Derby in June 1961.

Above: Nineteen-fifty-eight's dual-purpose 41-seaters on Tiger Cub chassis were bodied by Willowbrook. There were ten in the batch, from which No. **159** (**NRC 159**) is shown in a view taken at the Lawn Motor Park, Skegness, in August 1958.

Below: In 1958 twenty of the 1947 AEC Regals of the batch 752-94 had their chassis lengthened to 30ft and were fitted with new fully fronted dual-purpose 39-seat bodies by Willowbrook. They were then renumbered into a new series as 300-19. The vehicle shown is **RC 9694**, originally fleet number 788, that became **316** following the rebuild. It was photographed in August 1958 very soon after the work had been completed.

Above: In 1959 the rear-engined revolution had barely started, but Trent was early in the field with Leyland Atlanteans bodied to highbridge specification by MCCW or Roe and to lowbridge by Weymann, all ordered by the BET through the MCW sales organisation. Trent persevered with the Atlantean, and the slightly later Daimler Fleetline - despite undeniable reliability problems - and, unlike some operators, never thereafter bought any more new traditional front-engined double-deckers. Number **1080** (**RRC 80**), seen at Huntingdon Street in sparkling brand new condition, was a 1960 Roe-bodied delivery and was photographed in May of that year.

Below: A handy pairing of highbridge and lowbridge Atlanteans at Derby bus station in June 1961. Roe-bodied No. **1090** (**TCH 90**) on the left was a 1960 delivery and **1360** (**ORC 760**), bodied by Weymann, had entered the fleet in 1959. A further contrast is provided by 1948 AEC Regent No. **1154** (**ACH 644**) in use as a driver-training vehicle.

Above: The inexplicable withdrawal from AEC as chassis supplier resulting in an absence of new AECs in 1951-9 was corrected in 1960 with a batch of ten Reliances with 37-seat Fanfare coach bodies from Weymann. It is thought that the impression made by second-hand examples of the Reliance chassis, acquired with the Naylor fleet in 1956, brought the Southall manufacturer back into favour. Number **232** (**RRC 232**) was photographed in Sheffield in August 1961.

Below: Number **233** (**RRC 233**) of this batch suffered accident damage when still quite new and was rebodied by Harrington, as seen in this Huntingdon Street, Nottingham, view taken in June 1962.

Above: Standing out like a beacon, No. **41** (**VCH 241**)'s brightwork and predominantly cream livery contrast with the dull Huntingdon Street background on a May 1962 evening as passengers retrieve their luggage from the rear storage compartment. The 41-seat Seagull 70 coachwork was by Burlingham to the design that succeeded, but bore little or no resemblance to, the earlier Seagull style and the chassis was again an AEC Reliance. The vehicle was one of a batch of four.

Below: The Tiger Cub chassis from Leyland was retained for service buses and in March 1961 a batch of 15 with Willowbrook 45-seat bodywork was delivered. This Derby bus station scene from April 1963 includes No. **843** (**VCH 843**).

Above: **YRC 187**, with matching fleet number, was one of a batch of 20 Leyland Tiger Cub dual-purpose 41-seaters bodied by Alexander for 1962 delivery to Trent. It is seen alongside the Barton office at Huntingdon Street in June 1966.

Below: Another of the batch, No. **192** (**YRC 192**), was in the same spot some six years later, in March 1972. As so often, a pairing of Geoffrey Atkins's photographs records topographical detail changes over the years, as well - in this case - as a revised livery for the Trent vehicle.

Above: Reversed registrations appeared on Trent number plates in 1962 on a batch of ten Weymann-bodied highbridge 77-seat Leyland Atlanteans. From the batch 462-71 (62-71 ACH) we illustrate No. **71 (71 ACH)** at Derby bus station in October 1966.

Below: The need to separately order highbridge and lowbridge buses on the Leyland Atlantean chassis was mitigated somewhat with the introduction of the Daimler Fleetline, which did away with the sunken gangway and four-in-a-row seating necessary at the rear of the upper deck on the Atlantean. Superior Daimler drive-train and back-axle technology allowed coachbuilders to maintain conventional seating and a central gangway throughout the upper deck within a low-height configuration. Trent responded positively to this initiative with an order for ten in 1963. Number **624 (624 CCH)** at Derby in April 1963 demonstrates the carefully detailed Northern Counties 77-seat bodywork, whose styling was more attractive and less box-like than that of the MCW products.

Above: Twenty-four Leyland Leopards to the new 36ft maximum length (legal since July 1961) were bodied for Trent as dual-purpose 51-seaters by Willowbrook for delivery in 1963. The example chosen for our illustration, No. **220 (220 CCH)**, was at Huntingdon Street in September 1971. It was one of three of the batch (the others were 204 and 221) destroyed in the July 1976 fire at Derby.

Below: With the Leopard, Leyland regained Trent's orders for 30ft coaches for touring work. In 1964, a batch of five L2 models with Harrington 40-seater coachwork was delivered, of which No. **58 (ACH 58B)** is illustrated at Minehead, Somerset, in June 1965.

Above: Other Leyland Leopards in 1964 were 36ft-long examples in coach and service-bus form. The coaches were Alexander 49-seaters to that coachbuilder's classic Y-type design. In Geoffrey Atkins's regular portrait location, No. **229** (**ACH 229B**) was waiting to move onto the stand for a run to Manchester on the X2.

Below: The year's third variation on the Leyland Leopard was the Marshall-bodied 53-seat service bus, seen here at Derby bus station in August 1965 in the shape of No. **302** (**ACH 302B**). Legislation-driven Derby CBC year-letter suffix registrations were now in use on Trent vehicles after just over a year of the reversed variety: not long in comparison with authorities that had reversed their number series earlier.

Above: Plaxton's updated Panorama coach body had two features - the unnecessary bright mouldings and the visual separation of the first bay - that sat uneasily with the otherwise clean lines, a situation not resolved until the appearance of the Panorama Elite. The Plaxton design was nonetheless popular, and Trent took four with 49 seats on Leyland Leopard chassis in April 1965, one of which, No. **6** (**ECH 6C**), is seen at Huntingdon Street on excursion work when brand new.

Below: There could hardly have been a greater contrast between the Leopards and a batch of six Duple Bella Vega-bodied 41-seat Bedford SB5s also delivered in 1965. Standing in almost the same place, and also brand new, was No. **75** (**ECH 75C**), the last of the batch. The Bedfords did not last long and all had gone by 1972. They all found new owners in the independent sector.

Above: Number **251** (**ECH 251C**) was one of a large batch of Willowbrook-bodied dual-purpose vehicles. It was a 51-seater and is seen ahead of a Lincolnshire Bristol Lodekka at Huntingdon Street in June 1965 having been in service only since the preceding month.

Below: The Alexander Y-type coach body in short, 41-seat, form was specified for eight Leyland Tiger Cubs, which arrived in December 1965. The first of them, No. **100** (**HRC 100C**), was at Pennyfoot Street, Nottingham, in March 1967.

Above: The year 1965 was an interesting one for the Trent watcher, producing among all the varieties of Leyland and Bedford coach a batch of ten Daimler Fleetlines with Alexander 78-seat bodywork. Number **481 (ECH 481C)**, the last of the batch, is seen in a Union Street, Nottingham, view taken in March 1965.

Below: Weymann won the Trent order for 51-seat dual-purpose bodies to be mounted on a batch of ten Leyland Leopards for 1966 delivery. Difficulties at the Addlestone plant, however, caused its closure and the vehicles were transferred to the MCCW Elmdon plant for completion. In another portrait of a brand new vehicle, No. **261 (JRC 261D)** is seen in April 1965, the month of its delivery to Trent.

Above: The Alexander/Daimler Fleetline combination gave satisfaction and many more were ordered, including a batch of 20 in 1967. Number **498** (**MRC 498E**) is seen at Loughborough bus station in July 1973 alongside a superficially similar vehicle in the Midland Red fleet. The latter, however, had twin doorways and flat windscreen glass.

Below: **MRC 563E**, fleet number **563**, was a 1967 Leyland Leopard L2 with Plaxton 40-seat coachwork. It was one of a batch of five, all later repainted into National Bus Company white, as evidenced in this view at Nottingham Victoria in July 1975.

Above: Bedfords appeared again in 1967, when a small group of six VAM5 models for private hire work was delivered. Again not long-lived in the Trent fleet, they had gone by 1972. The Duple Viceroy coachwork was some two feet longer than that on the earlier Bedford SB5s, but retained the latter's 41-seat capacity. Number **81** (**MRC 581E**) was at Derby garage in April 1967.

Below: The cleaner lines of the Panorama Elite from Plaxton graced four Leyland Leopard 49-seat coaches at the beginning of 1969. Number **15** (**VCH 15G**) is seen in March 1973 at another favourite Geoffrey Atkins photography location - the loading bays at Nottingham Victoria.

Above: The pattern of buying batches of six cheap, lightweight Bedfords for mainly private hire use and selling them after five years or so continued in 1971 when the Bedford YRQ model with Plaxton 41-seat coachwork was chosen. Number **82** (**ERC 882J**) was the first of the batch. It was about six weeks old when photographed at Huntingdon Street, about to depart for Cromer, in July 1971.

Below: The first new Bristol in the Trent fleet was No. **343** (**LRC 343K**), one of a batch of five Eastern Coach Works-bodied RELL6Ls delivered in 1972. It was at Matlock bus station in July 1972. Withdrawn at the end of 1985, it eventually ended up running for Citybus in Belfast.

Above: The ability of Bristol and Eastern Coach Works to seek orders outside the state-owned companies brought about some interesting combinations, including in 1972 some ECW-bodied Daimler Fleetlines for Trent. Number **555 (NRC 55K)** is seen in bright, clean, brand new condition in Parliament Street, Nottingham, in July 1972 - doubtless on a Sunday.

Below: The transfer of a number of vehicles from the North Western fleet to Trent increased the latter's stock of Bristol RELLs, although the ex-North Western examples had 49-seat bodywork by Marshall, of Cambridge. Number **330 (SJA 345J)**, the former North Western No. 345, was at Matlock bus station in July 1972.

Above: The upheaval that brought North Western vehicles into the Trent fleet was quite wide-ranging and also saw Midland General stock transferred. Trent No. **169** (**29 DRB**), the former Midland General No. 260, was a Bristol MW6G Eastern Coach Works 43-seater that had been new in February 1958. It was also at Matlock bus station in July 1972.

Below: **569 ERR**, a 1961 ECW-bodied 60-seat Bristol FS6G Lodekka, moved across from Midland General to Trent as fleet number **665** in 1973. The vehicle had been new to Mansfield District, passing to Midland General in 1968.

Above: An ECW-bodied Bristol coming to Trent via a very different route, and somewhat later, was No. **760** (**SMS 37H**), a 1970 VRT/SL6G 70-seater that had been new to Alexander (Midland). Transferred to Eastern National in 1971 in exchange for an FLF Lodekka, it moved on to Crosville in 1982, passing eventually to Trent in 1987. The livery was a bizarre part-red, part-green concoction.

Below: The "six Bedfords" exercise was repeated again in 1973, resulting in Duple-bodied 41-seat YRQs. The last of them was No. **97** (**TCH 97L**), seen at Derby in June 1975.

Upper: Not all medium-capacity coaches were on the Bedford chassis. Number **39** (**YCH 900M**) was a Leyland Leopard PSU4B/4R, fitted with Plaxton 40-seat coachwork. It was photographed at Stockwell Gate, Mansfield, in May 1974.

Centre: The Leyland National was a phenomenon that was inevitable in a National Bus Company fleet and Trent's first examples arrived in 1974. The first of three in that year was No. **421** (**GNU 568N**), a 49-seater, seen at Derby in July 1976.

Lower: The following year the two-door variant of the National was tried. A batch of five such vehicles included No. **430** (**KVO 430P**), seen in unrelieved red livery at Nottingham Victoria in October 1975.

Above: Here is No. **430** (**KVO 430P**) again, at the same place but in March 1992, rebuilt to single-door specification and sporting the Ayres red and cream livery - the first Trent vehicle so turned out - that had been applied to it in October 1991.

Below: Number **575** (**ORB 575P**) was one of three Eastern Coach Works-bodied Leyland Atlantean AN68s among the huge Midland General to Trent transfer of October 1976. The photograph was taken at Derby in June 1990. The Midland General fleet had been fully renumbered into the Trent series in October 1972. This 1976 vehicle was thus numbered from new.

Upper: In February 1992 No. **575** (**ORB 575P**) went on loan to the Barton Buses fleet, by then under Trent control. Another Nottingham Victoria view, dating from November 1992.

Centre: A need was perceived for 35-seat service buses and in 1976 a pair of Bristol LHS6L chassis with Eastern Coach Works bodies were delivered. The second of them, No. **389** (**PNU 389R**) is seen at Trent's Derby Works in July 1978.

Lower: The Leyland Leopard/Alexander combination was still very much in favour with Trent in the mid 1970s. Number **108** (**PRA 108R**) was one of eight T-type 49-seat coaches delivered in 1976. It was at Matlock bus station in October 1977. All eight were reseated to 45 in 1977/8 and all but one reinstated as 49-seaters in 1981/5.

Above: Number **112** (**PRR 112R**) of the 1976 Alexander T types is seen in National Express livery at Derby in May 1984.

Below: Following the absorption of so many vehicles from North Western and Midland General, Trent was a major operator in the National Bus Company's portfolio. As might have been expected, orders for new vehicles included Bristol chassis as long as they were available. One of 1977's intake was No. **821** (**PVO 821R**), an ECW-bodied VRT/SL3/501 74-seater. It was photographed in Buxton during the short time that double-deckers were operated there. The date was June 1983 and the location outside Buxton Hospital. The service being worked was the cross-town 185 from Harpur Hill to Fairfield. Double-deckers used in Buxton did not have blinds for that route and usually showed "Town Service", although on occasion the destination was left blank. *(Ian Stubbs)*

Above: Prior to the demise of the Bristol vehicle-building operation at the hands of Leyland, Bristol had put in much of the development work on the VR double-decker's successor, which eventually emerged as the Leyland Olympian. Trent's first examples of the Olympian came in 1983 and No. **700** (**XAU 700Y**) - one of eight in that year - was the first of them all. It features in a May 1984 Derby bus station scene.

Below: In post-NBC days, Olympian No. **701** (**XAU 701Y**) was another example of the short-lived use of double-deckers in Buxton. It was at Bridge Street in April 1989, also on the 185 to Fairfield. Behind the bus is the Buxton depot of Trent, which has been replaced by that at Doveholes. The railway stock in the background is that of Peak Rail, who at that time had an operating base at the Buxton end of the former line to Matlock. *(Ian Stubbs)*

Above: Another new model to make its debut in the Trent fleet at around this time was the Leyland Tiger, in 1984. In National Holidays livery, Duple-bodied 50-seater No. **9** (**A709 CNU**) was leaving Nottingham Victoria in May of that year, having entered service the previous February.

Below: An unusual second-hand purchase in 1986 was of a pair of ex-London Transport Daimler Fleetlines that had been marketed when new in September 1976 as "Leylands". DMS1991/2019 in the LT fleet, they passed on sale by LT via a dealer to South Wales, of Swansea, being purchased by Trent in August 1986. As Nos **550/1**, **KJD 19P** and **KUC 991P** were at Derby soon after acquisition by Trent. Fitted with Metro-Cammell 76-seat bodywork, one had front upper-deck opening windows, the other did not. Trent withdrew them in July 1990.

Above: **E629 AMA** was an Iveco 49-10 that was new in 1988 as a demonstrator for the Carlyle Group, of Birmingham, who had built the bodywork. Originally a 21-seater, its capacity was increased to 25 for Trent service, from December 1988, as fleet number **50**. It ran for Trent until August 1993.

Below: Seen in Mansfield bus station in January 1989, having been delivered to Trent the previous month, is Volvo B10M-50 No. **600** (**F600 GVO**), an Alexander-bodied 84-seater. Eleven similar vehicles arrived in 1989. These were the first vehicles ordered after the Company had been privatised. The first eight, including this one, passed to Plymouth City Transport and the remaining four to Fingland's, Manchester, in 2000.

Above: Number **314** (**J314 BVO**), a DAF SB220LC550 with Optare 49-seat bodywork, was new to Trent in 1991, and was sold, along with seven others from the batch 309-25, to Barnsley & District in April 2002.

Below: On walks in recent years round his beloved Nottingham with Geoffrey Atkins, the writer always had a couple of Nikon F801 SLRs with him. Geoffrey had finally hung up his cameras and disbanded his dark room, selling off the equipment, a short time before we took just such a walk on 30th May 2001. Geoffrey, then 89 years old, kept eyeing the Nikons and his shutter finger was clearly twitching. Finally, he asked if he could "have a go" as, he explained, he had never owned a Nikon. Round his neck went the camera and with no hesitation at all - apart from a few "sighting shots" on a camera he had never handled before - his "eye was in" immediately and a fine series of afternoon rush-hour views in Mansfield Road resulted, including this view of No. **127** (**L127 LRA**) on its way to Hucknall. This Northern Counties-bodied 49-seat Volvo B10B-58 is one of a large batch delivered new to Trent in 1993/4.

Above: The high-profile TRANSPEAK leaving Nottingham for Manchester in May 1995. This view in Parliament Street is of No. **51** (**M51 PRA**), an Alexander Belfast dual-purpose 51-seater on a Volvo B10M-50 chassis, one of a batch of five delivered in 1994/5. By March 1999 they had been reseated to 47 and have only recently been withdrawn from Trent service. At the time of writing, they are being sold and are finding ready buyers; one has already gone to MK Metro and two to South Lancs, of Atherton.

Below: The modern midibus is perhaps most familiar in the shape of the Metrorider, built by Metro-Cammell and later by Optare, who acquired the rights to the design when Metro-Cammell closed. This Trent 31-seat example, No. **218** (**N218 VRC**), was new in October 1995. It was renumbered as 1218 in December 1999 and sold to Yorkshire Traction in September 2000. This picture at Nottingham Victoria was taken in February 1996.

Above: Optare also supplied bodywork and, indeed, marketed the complete vehicles as the Optare Sigma, for a batch of ten 46-seat Dennis Lances supplied in October 1995. This one is No. **358** (**N358 VRC**) leaving Victoria bus station, Nottingham, in November 1995. Starting in 1999, these vehicles were transferred to Notts & Derby; the latter has recently withdrawn the first two for sale.

Below: Another in the series taken by Geoffrey Atkins on 30th May 2001 in Mansfield Road recorded No. **901** (**P901 CTO**), a 1996 Plaxton-bodied 39-seat Dennis Dart SLF, on Barton's Calverton Connection in the reserved bus lane speeding into the centre of town. This is far from being the latest photography from this legend in his own lifetime, for he repeated this *tour de force* in March 2002. *(see page 58).*

Above: Once again tempted to take a few pictures - "for old times' sake" - during one of our walks around the streets close to his home, Geoffrey Atkins on 16th March 2002 took another excellent series of views, which included this look at Trent No. **245** (**Y268 DRC**), an Optare L1180 42-seater, in Rainbow 3 livery. Geoffrey was then eight weeks past his 90th birthday and his technique was as immaculate as ever. And even this is not his latest photography: he has subsequently - in February 2004 in Nottingham's Old Market Square - taken photographs of the new NET trams (again on one of the writer's cameras), thus becoming surely the only transport photographer to have recorded both Nottingham's original and 21st Century tramway systems: an achievement that quite delighted him.

Below: Geoffrey didn't take this one, but expressed a lively interest in this Calverton Connection-liveried vehicle, No. **631** (**FJ03 VWY**), a Wright-bodied 44-seat Scania L94UB, in Nottingham's Old Market Square, and asked that the photograph be taken. We had just come out of Debenhams having partaken of morning coffee, on 3rd September 2003, and Geoffrey was his usual entertaining self, in reminiscent vein about earlier, regulated, days, when none but Nottingham City Transport buses were permitted in the Old Market Square. *(John Banks)*

Appendix - Trainers, Demonstrators and Recovery Vehicles

Above: **LRC 454**, one of the 1958 Willowbrook-bodied Leyland Titan PD3/4 73-seaters, started its Trent service with the fleet number 1054. It was renumbered twice, as 420 and then 588, before being withdrawn from passenger service in 1977. In October of that year it was renumbered yet again, and as **A56** passed into the driver-training fleet, in which role it was photographed at Derby in July 1978. The vehicle is now preserved by Trent in its original red and ivory livery.

Below: Ex-Midland General Bristol FS6G Lodekka **569 ERR** *(see also page 46)* moved from passenger to driver-training service at the same time, taking the fleet number **A57**. It is also pictured at Derby, but in a June 1980 view.

Above: Number **A59** in the training fleet was **LCH 326K**, a Marshall-bodied Leyland Leopard 49-seater that had been new in 1972 as No. 326. It became a trainer in May 1981.

Below: Another 1981 move into the training fleet was that of Daimler Fleetline No. 925 (originally No. 525). The Alexander-bodied vehicle was thus renumbered as A61 and then as **T3**, its identity in this January 1983 picture at Derby.

Opposite page upper: Trent trainer No. **T5** (**MCN 831L**), an ex-Northern General Leyland National, is seen on training duties at Derby in May 1984.

Opposite page centre: Bristol VR trainer **T3** (**ORC 256N**) had been fleet number 784 in passenger service from 1974 to 1989. In this March 1990 view at Nottingham Victoria it was painted in a reversed livery.

Opposite page lower: Number **T1** (**YRC 181**) is a Leyland Leopard PSU3/3R with Alexander 53-seat bodywork. It was new to Alexander (Midland) as GLS 267N in 1974 and after a varied career joined the Trent fleet; it was reregistered YRC 181 in 1995, a number originally carried by a 1962 Trent Leyland Tiger Cub. The new YRC 181 was sold to the Nottingham independent Skills in September 1999 and passed into preservation in January 2004.

Above: In 1960 Trent borrowed a North Western Dennis Loline for evaluation. Nothing came of the trial; with hindsight, in view of Trent's commitment to the rear-engined concept, that hardly seems surprising. Number **818** (**RDB 818**) is seen arriving at Mount Street bus station, Nottingham, on service 8 from Derby, in May 1960.

Below: A similar trial, and one that had a more positive outcome, was of Birmingham Corporation's Daimler Fleetline No. **3246** (**246 DOC**), seen running for Trent - again at Mount Street on the Derby to Nottingham service 8 - in March 1962.

Upper: **K170 FYG**, a DAF DB250LB50J, bodied by Optare as a 74-seater, was built in 1992. It was tried out by Trent in June 1993 and is seen leaving Victoria bus station, Nottingham.

Centre: The DAF/Optare combination featured again on **J365 BNW**, seen inside Victoria in October 1993 on trial for Trent. An SB220LC550 chassis, the bodywork had 49 seats.

Lower: In April 1995, and again photographed as it was leaving Nottingham Victoria, Wright-bodied 51-seat Volvo B10B-58 was demonstrated to Trent.

Service stock, or non-PSV as they were once known, are a fascinating adjunct to bus company operations, especially when the vehicles are converted former buses or coaches. That was not the case with these Trent recovery wagons, although the six-wheeler does have a frontal treatment that would not have looked out of place on a Bristol RE single-decker. The photographs were taken at Meadow Road garage, Derby, in November 1976 *(above)* and September 1979. The 1976 view shows the building damaged after the fire the previous July. The vehicles are all AECs: the six-wheeler, fleet number **A16**, being a 1953 ex-military AEC Militant; the other two (from right to left) were **A18/7**, AEC Mandators dating from 1972/69, and acquired by Trent in 1979/8.